IN THE COMPANY OF NARCISSISTS: SOMEBODY ALWAYS PAYS

KIMBERLY A. TAYLOR

All characters appearing in this work are fictitious. Any resemblance to real persons, living or dead – even those based on real people (which should be plainly apparent to them and those who know them) is purely coincidental.

ISBN-10:0692433856
ISBN-13: 9780692433850

DEDICATION

To my loving husband Chuck, our two rescue dogs Captain Jacques & Princess Cinderella and noble kitten Sir Didier Erasmus II

FRONT COVER

Hypocrisy comes far too often disguised as a prophet.

The veiled prophet----like the one on the cover---came to represent wealth, honor and philanthropy. Dreamed up by a grain broker and former Confederate cavalryman, the prophet (chosen from among the city's elite and always kept secret) hosted a parade and a ball in St. Louis, starting in 1878 and lasting for some 135 years.

Taken from a poem by Thomas Moore "The Veiled Prophet of Khorassan" published in 1871, the "VP Fair" as it came to be known had a fairy tale quality about it, complete with Mardi Gras style floats.

St. Louis area residents were spellbound.

For the founders, all white businessmen and civic leaders from St. Louis, it served as a way not only to revitalize St. Louis' Agricultural and Mechanical Fair, which drew thousands, but also to teach a lesson about the importance of social hierarchy.

People turned out and tuned into the VP Parade and lived vicariously through the annual debutante ball, during which a "Queen of Love and Beauty" was crowned.

Families whose bread and butter came from the unions, whose families were union leaders, were encouraged to watch the spectacle---even though the VP parade had replaced those organized by workers' unions. In fact, the whole affair was organized after a labor strike, the Great Railroad Strike of 1877, which involved not only white but African American workers. The first VP was the Police Commissioner, who just happened to suppress the 1877 strikers---who attempted to stop anyone from taking the jobs vacated by them.

Enter civil and women's rights and so much for the racist and sexist underpinnings. On Dec. 22, 1972, one woman, a member of a local civil rights group, actually slid down from a power cable in Keil Auditorium and unmasked the Prophet---St. Louis based Monsanto Company executive VP Tom K. Smith.

What a match made in heaven. No one is better suited to false advertising than Monsanto. The society created a myth. They sold the idea of their prophet as benevolent. The Veiled Prophet of Khorassan was benevolent for the simple reason that they said he was. What started as a war mongering trickster was turned into a mystic traveler who decided to make St. Louis his home. That's the power of suggestion.

The original poem served as inspiration for this mystic traveller, as the following excerpt demonstrates, taken from Moore's Lalla Rookh: An Oriental Romance:

On either side, with ready hearts and hands, His chosen guard of bold Believers stands; Young fire-eyed disputants who deem their swords, On points of faith, more eloquent than words...What dazzling mimicry of God's own power Hath the bold Prophet planned to grace this hour?

CONTENTS

To understand a thing, you must first name it. - Socrates

Narcissist: A narcissist is someone who not only thinks he or she is always right but, at the expense of others' welfare, will defend violently and vehemently his or her point of view. Narcissists sacrifice others, not themselves, in pursuit of what they want. They feel they are superior and do not hesitate to put others down.

When threatened, a narcissist points a finger of blame at the accuser. Narcissists are despicable characters. They lie because they do not have a conscience to keep themselves from lying. Some might say they are so self-deluded as to believe their own lies - their own tainted view of the world, the world according to a narcissist.

Narcissists are the worlds' foremost abusers. Unfortunately, they do not work alone. They have help from others, who are either equally narcissistic or are so easily led around that they fall prey to their will. Believing that this bestows power of some kind does not change the narcissist's purpose. Narcissists value others only in

1

terms of themselves and as an extension of themselves.

At the very least, narcissists are scam artists. Those who believe and follow narcissistic leaders are weak minded and are easily conned into believing that, at least on some level, the narcissist will take care of them. They are willing to ignore the abusive treatment of other living creatures for their own sake. They will be kept in their company only as long as the narcissist views them as useful and they gain from the relationship.

That is how abusive practices take hold and spread. They grow in proportion to the number willing to ignore the cost born by the exploited. Fair trade is one response to the world's unceasing ability to turn a blind eye to exploitation and poisoning of the environment.

Shine a light, different from the one the narcissist is hogging, and you'll uncover the world's ills, if not ill-gotten gains.

Human rights and animal rights are closely tied. They both depend on a greater degree of empathy than many are willing to give. From animal cruelty to human exploitation to environmental concerns, these abhorrent violations of basic dignity are on the rise around the world.

Kimberly A. Taylor

Narcissist: A narcissist is someone who not only thinks he or she is always right but, at the expense of others' welfare, will defend violently and vehemently his or her point of view.

Beyond Blood Diamonds---

When diamonds have helped fund civil wars in Africa, they are commonly referred to as blood or "conflict" diamonds. Even though wars in places like Angola and Sierra Leone are now over, the mining of diamonds in rebel-held areas still goes on.

The process, meant to curtail the sale and export of "conflict" diamonds, is known as the Kimberley Process (named for the Kimberley, South Africa mines). It is only partially successful. Some might say it has failed entirely.

As with most well-meaning human rights efforts, it ultimately falls upon the consumer to decide what "conflict free" certification means. Often, due to loopholes, the certification is no more meaningful than the words "free range" or "cage free" on a carton of eggs.

Instead, what it does mean is just the opposite - that they are obtained in inhumane conditions. It is up to us to uphold basic dignity no matter what the commodity happens to be.

Animal Furs

Examples include South African Zulus whose customs dictate the use of animal pelts, specifically leopard pelts, in their rituals. Well-meaning outsiders have tried to replace the actual skins with a synthetic version, a faux fur if you will, for sale to the group.

The material has not proven to be of high enough quality to pass muster with the tribal group. Also, it has seemed a better solution for them to reuse old skins for the sake of their intrinsic value, or nostalgia, and their extrinsic beauty, natural of origin.

Sustainability dictates principles of reuse, repurpose and recycle. The tribal members' argument is that the pelts last over twenty years. It's hard to fault them on that point.

I'm a firm believer in finding multiple uses for the things I already own. I also prefer quality over quantity. Quality lasts longer.

If we're smart, we'll have fewer discards---and in this throw-away society---that's a major undertaking in terms of re-education.

I do not own a fur, so I won't have to deal with this particular dilemma. However, the ongoing problem facing the Shembe is that their numbers are increasing. Poaching of leopards is on the rise because of the tradition of elders within the religion---a combination of Christian (Baptist) and Zulu culture---requiring elders to wear leopard pelts as a sign of wealth and honor.

Although I disagree on principle with the slaughter of animals for the use of their fur, it's too bad there aren't enough traditional ceremonial pelts to go around since efforts to develop a suitable replacement have not yet gained ground.

Factory Fires, Locked Doors and Other Corporate Nightmares

Reminiscent of the Triangle Shirtwaist Factory fire in NYC, another incident in China brings to light the high human costs of China's lax industrial safety standards. Workers at the poultry factory, known as Jhin Baoyuanfeng Poultry Plant, struggled through smoke and flames only to reach doors that were blocked and locked. At least 120 were lost. The incident occurred on June 1, 2013.

About 100 years earlier, on March 25, 1911, the Triangle Shirtwaist factory fire in NYC led to safety standards reforms in the U.S. It was also because managers had locked doors to stairwells and exits that many workers could not escape and ended up jumping from 8th, 9th and 10th floors. According to reports I've read, around 146 died as a result.

Now, let's turn to the Tazreen Fashion Factory outside Dhaka Bangladesh. Again, due to locked doors at this garment factory, at least 117 were killed. This incident, like the one in China, occurred only recently, on November 24, 2012.

It shouldn't surprise us that such incidents occur in plants that have at their very core, perhaps their core competency, something to do with slaughter and greed. With Christmas just around the corner, recognizable corporate giants and world renowned name brands such as Wal-Mart and Sears, not to mention France's Carrefour, as well as other European based multi-nationals, were rushing to make deadlines. Disney labels, as well as Tommy Hilfiger and The Gap were found amongst the debris.

Narcissists sacrifice others, not themselves, in pursuit of what they want. They feel they are superior and do not hesitate to put others down.

A Rite Of Passage

Garment factories have a long, sordid history. In April 2012, more than 1,000 workers were killed when the Rana Plaza factory building in Bangladesh collapsed.

Even though the cotton might come from a field in Mississippi, the long journey involved in the manufacturing of a garment as simple as a T-shirt is astounding. Such revelations were made apparent in a PBS series following the life of a t-shirt as part of a study inspired by Pietra Rivoli's book: "The Travels of a T-Shirt in the Global Economy" and spearheaded by co-founder of Planet Money, Adam Davidson.

The manufacturing takes place where labor is not only abundant but very, very cheap. In fact the garment industry is known for following poverty. The overriding excuse used in industry circles to justify such practices is that it is only a rite of passage that every developing country must go through. That's more like a marriage of convenience than one of commitment. Nonetheless, many countries have gone through "the t-shirt phase" considered to be a step in the ladder of economic development.

Bangladesh became a favorite for the garment industry, now perhaps more of a poster child, when Richard Nixon set out to develop a global agreement, the MFA (or Multifiber Arrangement) that set quotas on the amounts of clothing other countries could export to the U.S. Since South Korea had its quota, it gave incentives for Korean businessmen to set up shop someplace else, such as Bangladesh.

About four million people work in the garment industry in Bangladesh. They make more than they did on subsistence farms and they make more than without the industry's presence; but they are paid low wages by anyone's standards, which hardly makes it ethical.

The question is whether Bangladesh is unique in that its apparel exports make up a bigger share of Bangladesh's overall exports than they historically did for any of the other countries looked at, to name a few: China, South Korea and Japan. In those countries, the textiles and apparel

industry brought in manufacturing and invest-
ment knowledge which translated into higher
level industries (such as electronics). So far, no
country is ready to replace Bangladesh as the
cheapest place in the world to make clothes.
Even with a near doubling of the minimum
wage, they'll still be the lowest wage country of
the top 20 clothing exporters worldwide.

Sustainability in the Garment Industry

The sustainability question is also one that
needs to be addressed. What are the environmental impacts of large amounts of pesticides
and water used for growing cotton, not to mention the effects in terms of carbon footprint of
the 20,000 miles the T-shirt traveled around the
world from a U.S. cotton field through the manufacturing process in countries like Bangladesh
and Colombia (where they make four times the
wages and have better working conditions) and,
finally, back to the U.S. as a finished product.

Most of the work leading up to the spinning into
yarn or thread, which takes place in Indonesia
before going to Bangladesh, and the sewing,

which takes place in Columbia and Bangladesh, is automated. The top reason that the U.S. exports more cotton than any other country worldwide is technology. Interestingly, the process involves genetically modified crops.

Usually, genetically modified seeds are controversial but seemingly not among American cotton farmers. Approximately 90% of cotton grown in the U.S. is derived from genetically modified seeds, designed in labs and resistant to pests. Technology plays an even greater part in the process, as a John Deere picker needs only one operator vs. the five it took only a couple of years ago, and that one operator barely needs to touch the wheel to pick 100 acres of cotton a day.

Because the USDA tests all 17 million bales of cotton harvested in the U.S., report cards exist on levels of how fine, long, strong and bright white every single batch of cotton is so that cotton buyers around the world know exactly what they are getting. Even though farmers pay for the testing, they are subsidized in other ways. Crop insurance, in the form of revenue insurance, pays farmers if they make less than expected. In addition, they get payments when prices fall and, at least in the past, even got direct payments when prices were going through the roof.

Should it be any surprise who supplies the seeds...it's our old friend Monsanto.

Narcissists are the worlds' foremost abusers. Unfortunately, they do not work alone. They have help from others, who are either equally narcissistic or are so easily led around that they fall prey to their will. Believing that this bestows power of some kind does not change the narcissist's purpose. Narcissists value others only in terms of themselves and as an extension of themselves.

Seeds and Greed

Adding insult to injury, Monsanto's patent infringement cases further contribute to the bad taste left in our mouths from their GMOs.

In his documentary, "Bitter Seeds," filmmaker Micha X. Peled accuses Monsanto's GM seeds as a cause of farmer suicides in India.

Monsanto's non-renewable seeds have forced many farmers in India to the point of bankruptcy.

They cannot afford to buy a new batch every year.

Plus, Monsanto's seeds require more water and fertilizers than the farmers can provide.

Monsanto's aggressive marketing has resulted in a phase out of local varieties of seeds in many parts of India.

The backstory concerns Monsanto's patented seeds. The fact is that their genetically modified seeds are protected by patents. Farmers who grow GM crops must buy new seeds each year and cannot use traditional seed saving practices.

St. Louis based Monsanto, aka MonSatan, has maintained that it does not sue farmers whose crops are inadvertently contaminated by its GM seeds.

That's what they say, and unfortunately too many people believe them. However, according to the Center for Food Safety (a nonprofit group based in Washington, DC), Monsanto annually investigates approximately 500 farmers for possible patent infringement. Cases I've read include both those in the U.S. and Canada. The same report says that Monsanto sued 144 farmers from 1997-2010.

The Dirty Dozen: A Justification

My suspicion all along has been that they are out to justify their dirty little secrets by claiming or pretending their GMOs are actually a kind of fortified food coming from super seeds out to save the world. Never fear, Monsanto is here! Since when is more of a bad thing a good solution?

With a list of products that poison consumers headed by what has become known as the Dirty Dozen behind them, who in their right mind wouldn't believe their rhetoric.

Monsanto has taken the term "unenlightened self-interest" to new heights pretending that it is just the opposite. They claim to be enlightened by practicing the old "doing well by doing good" kind of self-interest. It's hard to believe that their quest to go after farmers around the world isn't in their best interests alone, with total disregard for the interests of the farmers or those they might feed.

It's just too bad it isn't true that their pursuits aren't less selfish, opportunistic or, in a word, narcissistic. Who wouldn't want a do-gooder multi-national corporation helping to feed the world in their pursuit of "enlightened self-interest."

For the Betterment of Humanity

Mahatma Ghandi is quoted as having said: "The greatness of a nation can be judged by the way its animals are treated."

Monsanto's Dirty Dozen includes, among its products produced throughout its existence as a corporation, those which are harmful both to humans and to animals. There is an interconnectedness in nature that Monsanto is clearly abusing and violating with decisions that are far from goodness.

The following list bears this point out well:

1. Saccharin: Sweet n' Low
2. PCB's
3. Polystyrene
4. Atom bomb and nuclear weapons
5. DDT
6. Dioxin
7. Agent Orange
8. Petroleum based fertilizer
9. Round Up
10. Aspartame (NutraSweet/Equal)
11. Bovine Growth Hormone
12. Genetically Modified Crops/GMOs

The majority of Monsanto's profits are from seeds engineered to tolerate Monsanto's Round Up, which is an ever rising dual income stream, as weeds continue to evolve resistance to Round Up.

As for the Bovine Growth Hormone, this genetically modified hormone was developed by Monsanto to be injected into dairy cows to produce more milk. Cows subjected to it (rBGH) suffer excruciating pain due to swollen udders. The rBGH milk has been linked to breast and colon cancer as well as to prostate cancer in humans.

At the very least, narcissists are scam artists. Those who believe and follow narcissistic leaders are weak minded and are easily conned into believing that, at least on some level, the narcissist will take care of them. They are willing to ignore the abusive treatment of other living creatures for their own sake. They will be kept in their company only as long as the narcissist views them as useful and they gain from the relationship.

Blunders In the Name of Science

Persuading large groups of people via the use of authority and in the name of science, or for the betterment of humanity, is nothing new.

When it comes down to personal gain rather than humanitarian goals, then it falls under the auspices of not only opportunism but also of outright narcissism, a truly devilish pursuit.

It pains me to even write about such atrocities as animal cruelty in the name of science. The following stories are an example of such a sinister case:

<u>"Apology to Elephants" amendment</u>

After some hesitation, I watched HBO's documentary, "An Apology to Elephants." I say hesitation only because watching animal abuse is always painful, even when presented as a public "wake-up" call.

I had a funny feeling the story of Thomas Edison electrocuting an elephant, as described in my post: "<u>The Light Bulb Effect or Electroshock or Just Plain Shock,</u>" would make its way into the

23

documentary...and it did. David Weigand describes the attention grabbing scene in his recent review of the film:

Should we fault the film for failing to present "the other side" of the argument? Perhaps, but it's difficult to imagine much justification for the images we've seen of baby elephants being hogtied, prodded and slapped into submission by trainers. It's especially difficult when we learn of one elephant's contribution to scientific advancement, at the hands of none other than Thomas Edison. In 1903, a famous elephant named Topsy was not only an audience favorite at Coney Island Amusement Park, but also a useful work animal as well, until she went rogue. Over time, she killed three of her trainers. The last time, she reacted when the trainer tried to jam a lit cigarette in her mouth. Just 28, relatively young for an elephant, she was ordered to be euthanized. Edison stepped in and offered to do the job, which he filmed as "Electrocuting the Elephant." The film still exists and is included in the HBO film. We watch the moment when the current surges through the elephant and she falls instantly to the ground.

The execution of Topsy is disturbing to watch. What is also disturbing and left out of the narration was Edison's opportunistic-narcissistic motive for performing the execution, which had nothing to do with "scientific advancement," as history would have us believe.

<u>Truly just as shocking...The Light Bulb Effect or Electroshock or just plain shock?</u>

Here's another instance of history rewarding the wrong person, another devil in disguise.

I feel I've been cheated by having received only half an education. For example, all I learned about Edison in grade school is that he was credited with the invention of the light bulb. In fact, he was a diabolical character, which did not make its way into my textbooks.

Let's shine the light on Edison beginning with his relationship with Nikola Tesla, a one time employee and someone whose work outshined Edison's ACHIEVEMENTS.

We need to teach our children the backstory. This story has more to do with con artistry than science, the old dog and pony show, with an unfortunately cruel twist.

Edison not only did an injustice to Tesla but also committed atrocities to innocent animals to try to prove his point. In an attempt not to lose control over his turf—his DC empire—he started by having fliers printed warning about the dangers of Tesla's AC.

Unfortunately, it did not end there.

If there is not a special place in hell, well you know what I mean.

His demonstration involved placing two wires onto an animal, sometimes an elephant, and speaking to the dangers of AC by energizing the two wires.

He achieved his unconscionable effect by causing: concern among the crowd of onlookers of what would surely be dangers if they used it at home; electrocution of the poor animal who fell into a heap; and the smell of burning flesh just to add the right touch to his cruel exhibit.

It's about time we start shining the light on others of his kind.

That is how abusive practices take hold and spread. They grow in proportion to the number willing to ignore the cost born by the exploited.

The Milgram Experiment

In the 1960's, psychologist Stanley Milgram conducted experiments at Yale University dealing with the very subject of "evil" deeds.

First, here's a brief description of the experiment. The subject, called a "teacher" is given directives (or orders) from an "experimenter," to inflict what the former believes are painful electric shocks to a "learner," who is actually an actor. The subject believes that for each wrong answer, in a word pair game, the learner was receiving actual electric shocks. In reality, there were no such punishments for wrong answers. Pre-recorded sounds for various shock levels were played for effect.

Simply put, this experiment is a study in obedience to an authority figure. Whereas Edison used Topsy to convince an audience of the dangers of Tesla's AC, the Milgram Experiment was done in the name of science in order to deal with the Holocaust question, generally speaking: Were Nazis really criminals or simply soldiers following orders?

It was found later that the subjects used in the Milgram Experiment reported and exhibited high degrees of stress for as long as they continued with the experiment. This was considered by some to be a human rights violation. The common thread is the use or abuse of humans and/or animals to prove a point in the name of science. It also has a lot to say about how we respond to authority, whether it means trusting a scientist like Edison, who was only out to disprove a rival, not to save the world from danger; or whether it involves the use of a scientist giving orders to a subject in order to prove that Nazis were only following orders, rather than acting on some kind of motive of hatred for the Jews.

The strong influence that idealism of scientific enquiry has on volunteers is apparent in both the original and several subsequent stagings of the experiment, which over the years have become less frequent as the overall population learns of the experiment. Only a quarter of the participants refused to continue to the end in 2009 when replicated in an episode of the BBC science documentary series Horizon. In the

2010 French documentary, Le Jeu de la Mort
(The Game of Death), only 16 out of 80 chose to
end the game before administering the highest
possible voltage.

The experiment was found to be inapplicable to
Holocaust crimes. Subjects were told that no
permanent physical damage would result from
their actions. (Holocaust perpetrators knew
their actions would result in physical damage.)

Subjects of the study were also not motivated
by racism as Holocaust perpetrators were.

The experiment lasted a mere hour compared to
the Holocaust which lasted for years. The goal
was set well beforehand and there was ample
time for moral assessment or reassessment of
authority---both in terms of organizations and
individuals involved.

It is simply an experiment in obedience to
measure the willingness of study participants to
obey an authority figure (first performed in
1961) who instructed them to perform acts that
would conflict with their personal conscience.
Specifically, it was meant to answer: "Was it

that Eichmann and his accomplices in the Holocaust had mutual intent?" In other words, were all Nazis in agreement with their superiors or were they simply following orders?

Although some found the experiment to be in violation of subjects' human rights, many subjects were reported to respond with gratitude for what the experiment taught them---not to obey individuals simply because they were in a position of authority.

Ponerology: The Science of Evil (or Evil is as Evil does)

Is it still evil even if it lacks evil intent?

As the Milgram Experiment demonstrated, a majority of non-pathological people went against their own instincts to comply with the orders of the authority figure who directed them to inflict greater and greater voltage.

Overall, two-thirds of participants were willing to administer maximum voltage.

An equal number, 90% of participants, were willing to do it if they saw someone else willing do it first; but they refused to do it if they saw someone else refuse to do it first. That's the good news.

If the pack mentality works, it can work for good as easily as it can work for evil. It is for this very reason that those who are "in the know" should resist the influence of the wrong kind of leadership. Strength in numbers means not only physical strength but perhaps more importantly psychological strength.

The example of the Nazi hierarchy is a classic for demonstrating how pathological people can and do rise to power and influence many. It is a frightening example, but it is unfortunately not the only example.

Businesses as well as governments fall into the trap of a follow-the-leader mentality. Such leaders as those erode little by little (as if by degree of voltage) the ethics we were taught as children. It is as if growing up we are trained to learn a new doctrine, a far less kind approach to the treatment of nature, of animals and of humankind, all in the name of progress.

Empathy is lacking among the pathological. It is replaced by narcissism. Those with a high degree of narcissism, who fall into the type known as NPD, narcissistic personality disorder, ignore the feelings of others in their decision making.

The trick is to prevent them from exerting more influence, to learn to resist their influence, and to educate how to avoid falling into the wrong mentality before it's too late.

It's just the way things are (or if you can't beat 'em, join 'em) is a poor excuse for not changing the system.

Again, the rise to power of Hitler and his inner circle is just one example (albeit a very strong example) of how a few pathological people can shape systems that drive behaviors that mirror their own pathological values---and, in turn, create structures within the society that perpetuate their behaviors. A vicious cycle of behavior leading to structure that can create behavior in others simply because they are in positions of power makes me shudder.

Such influences lead to decisions away from goodness. It falls on anyone who sees such influences to eradicate them and thus to keep them away from positions of power.

There is always another way.

Obedience versus Rebellion

Increasingly severe statements, such as: "The experiment requires that you continue," were enough to urge 65%, approximately two-thirds, of the "teachers" to progress to maximum voltage level in the original Milgram experiment. This is just the opposite of what Milgram expected. The type of response Milgram expected as the norm was for the majority to refuse to continue. Although some teachers did refuse early on, despite urging from the experimenter, they were in the minority.

The following commands were given in this order anytime the subject expressed desire to stop the experiment:

1) Please continue.

2) The experiment requires that you continue.

3) It is absolutely essential that you continue.

4) You have no other choice, you must go on.

Given such commands, more were willing to continue, even to the point of one who repeated to himself: "It's got to go on; it's got to go on."

More willingness to continue occurred when:

1) The authority figure was in close proximity;

2) Teachers felt they could pass on responsibility to others;

3) The experiment took place under the auspices of a respectable organization.

As some participants were debriefed following the experiment, they showed great relief at finding the student had not been harmed by them. One is even reported to have cried thinking he had killed him.

The question that baffles many is why did anyone obey? What was in it for them, or what did they fear as a repercussion if they did not continue?

This issue has been dealt with by examining the difference between those who obeyed and those who rebelled by dividing them into three categories:

1) Obeyed but justified themselves. They transferred blame onto either the experimenter (who was in charge) or the learner (who was so stupid and stubborn he deserved it). The underlying idea was that the learner was deliberately not thinking hard enough about the learning experience and thus deserved punishment.

2) Obeyed but blamed themselves. Those who fell into this category---if faced with similar circumstances in the future--- would be more likely to rebel. They were quite harsh on themselves, as they felt very bad (and responsible) for what they had done. Such teachers were apt to encourage learners to please think very carefully before answering so as to avoid further punishment.

3) Rebelled. Those who were in this category felt they were accountable to a

higher power or authority---a greater ethical imperative calling for protection of the learner over the experimenter. They not only questioned such authority, but they also held their ground and argued their right to disobey the authority figure.

Why so few rebelled is still a mystery except to say that obedience seems to be so entrenched in some people that it supersedes even personal codes of conduct. There is also the question of appearances in terms of acting in cooperation with authority.

Either way it's scary.

We trust scientists because we believe science is good or at least that it has as an ultimate goal to produce something good for humanity. That's what Monsanto and other multi-nationals are counting on, too. Progress comes at a price and somebody always pays.

The question not being asked is why trust them? At whose expense do such groups seek to produce something they deem as good for humanity?

Let's define "good" from their angle. A narcissist's take or perspective on what is good is: whatever is good for them is good for all.

There's unfortunately no shortage of narcissistic people in the world of business or politics.

When threatened, a narcissist points a finger of blame at the accuser. Narcissists are despicable characters. They lie because they do not have a conscience to keep themselves from lying. Some might say they are so self-deluded as to believe their own lies - their own tainted view of the world, the world according to a narcissist.

Politics Makes Strange Bedfellows: You Can't Make a Silk Purse from a Sow's Ear

Speaking of narcissists, most people have heard of Rod "Blago" Blagojevich, former governor of Illinois (which just happens to be my home state as well as my husband's). He used to make guest appearances on various TV shows like some sort of side show performer, bungee jumping off tall buildings in a single bound. I got so tired of seeing this criminal make an even bigger buffoon of himself than he already was, nothing pleased me more than when he was finally taken from the big top to the big house.

Quel cirque, as the French would say.

But, there's more to the story than meets the eye, as Blago was not without his minions. Like attracts like in love and war and most especially it seems in politics. In particular, this story involves corrupt Chicago politics.

Like some sort of Frankenstein, Blago was not without his very own monster, a creature named Christopher Kelly.

So, who was Chris Kelly? For starters, he was a college classmate of my husband's at the University of Illinois. They were in the same program together - Landscape Architecture.

He'd come around the workroom right before a project was due looking for ideas from those who'd been working diligently from the start. He'd burst in loudly and abruptly demand: "What are you doing? What are you doing? What are you doing?"

His frat brother, Martin Kiesewetter, said he remembered Kelly's room where he had all sorts of architectural drawings up on his wall. No doubt those drawings were based on ideas he stole from others in the landscape architecture program.

Once a Crook, Always a Crook...

With people like Kelly, there are no boundaries. He was not simply confident. He was outright cocky. He was not just driven. He was a criminal. He was a cheat. He was a rat.

If his frat brothers ever reported differently, it must be because they were just like him.

Of course, many saw him as my husband did. Many who worked with him later in life saw him just as my husband did. He did not, as one former insider suggested, take his own life rather than "rat out a friend." He was a rat who was trapped and who, like Hitler, took the coward's way out.

So, what led to this particular rat, who fittingly and ironically took rat poison, to end his own life?

As the story goes, it was on September 11, 2009, when the tough-talking Christopher Kelly, high roller from Champaign, a guy who bullied and cheated his way to the top of Illinois politics — Rod Blagojevich's campaign manager, took a lethal cocktail of aspirin, Tylenol PM and rat poison. He was part of Blagojevich's inner-most circle. They were as crooked a pair of politicians as any the state of Illinois has ever known.

I doubt very much that he did himself in rather than rat out a friend. Sure Kelly was scheduled to testify on his old boss, but he was also facing a lengthy prison term of his own.

Let's take a closer look at Kelly's lifestyle before and after being arraigned on racketeering and extortion charges related to the indictment of then Governor Rod Blagojevich.

His marriage was all but over. In between shacking up in a downtown Chicago condo with his girlfriend, Clarissa Flores-Buhelas, married and decades younger, he was holing up in a trailer near 173rd and Cicero.

That's worlds away from his many gabled and fabled Burr Ridge mansion which now had a $2.1 million foreclosure on it. Add to that his roofing company was finished and officials had banned him from doing business ever again with the City of Chicago.

So much for certain misguided and crooked politicians who thought he'd killed himself in the name of loyalty and love. There's more than one narcissist in this story because only a narcissist would think this way: "He'd rather take his own life than rat out a friend."

Hitler killed himself when he knew his empire was over and he was caught.

I'm not sure whether Hitler had any second thoughts but Kelly did. He sent a text message to his girlfriend to: "Come get me asap yard." We can only assume he did not want to die after all and, if he hadn't died, he would have had to testify against his crony as well as pay for his own crimes.

It's reported to have been an ugly scene. No one does that sort of thing to themselves unless they are desperate about their own circumstances.

The feds had indicted him three times in two years. He had pled guilty twice and was slated to go on trial with Blago on a third set of charges. A decade or more of prison loomed before him. He had even admitted to reporters four days earlier: "My life is over."

The pills took hold. He was violently ill, first vomiting inside the trailer, then outside. He was shoeless as he stumbled onto the gravel. He made it to his Cadillac Escalade where he threw up again inside. Simply clad in a T-shirt and jeans, covered in feces and puke, the former power broker was carrying a Wal-Mart bag filled with more pills.

He actually managed to drive himself to the parking lot of the Forest Lumber store, where Flores-Buhelos was racing to save him.

Once again, it sounds like he wanted to be saved, but it was too late.

So what's the back story?

The reality is that his whole life story was based on lies. Narcissists are born liars and Kelly was classic for his type.

He was not from humble, blue collar beginnings as he so often presented himself. Instead, he grew up in a large Irish Catholic family who were well off enough to belong to the Champaign Country Club, a posh place especially for those days. All seven children in the family attended prestigious colleges, including Notre Dame and, as previously mentioned, in Kelly's case, the University of Illinois.

When Blago and Kelly met, it was love at first sight. They hit it off because of their similar "ethnic" backgrounds. Blago liked Kelly because he came across as a blue collar neighborhood guy, who loved sports and could talk stats with him. But, most of all, he could raise the money.

With his fast talking and high flying attitude, he even managed to muscle out Blago's own father-in-law by shattering previous records and helping him win the Democratic nomination for governor in 2002, by raising more than $30 million.

Despite this marriage made in heaven, the relationship proved disastrous for both Blago and Kelly in the end.

Contracts Kelly won, especially for O'Hare Airport, were suspect. How did he beat out his competitors by so much? For example, it perplexed Bill O'Brien, VP of Combined Roofing Services in West Chicago: "We were one of three roofing companies that bid on a...contract out at O'Hare probably six, seven, eight years ago...We did our calculation, and we ended up at $10 million. We get the bid results and he's at $2 million, and we're scratching our heads [wondering] what the hell's going on here. We then bid another similar contract three years later. We screwed down our numbers tighter and tried to be a little more aggressive, and we still got blown away. He got it again. So, we asked ourselves: 'How's he doing that?'"

Of course, they had suspicions Kelly was cheating.

Nonetheless, some were taken in by Kelly, even to the point of thinking that he never had any hidden agenda.

Other smarter folks recognize a narcissist when they meet one. Whether they knew to call Kelly a narcissist or not, they knew he was a far more sinister character. This was always my husband's opinion.

It seems those who worked closely with Kelly fell into two camps: those he could easily fool (or were just like him) and those who knew him for a cheat and who, quite understandably, could not stand him.

I especially like the comment made by one current member of the Springfield, IL, legislature: "He seemed fascinated by politics and fancied himself as a big political thinker and player. To me, he was a heavy-handed braggart. I think he thought he was the power behind the throne."

A Crass Bully and a Blowhard...

He played wise guy and that's dangerous because guys who play wise guy and think they understand stuff they don't understand always get into trouble. Loud, opinionated, obnoxious are all adjectives used to describe him by a former senior aide.

Dangerous is a pretty strong descriptor. Just how dangerous became clear to everyone present at a meeting one day. It was reported by the same former senior aide:

"We were in the campaign office, and we were trying to make the point that we need to be careful who we take money from. And Kelly stands up and he's yelling, pointing to the finance office next door, and he's like: 'I built a fundraising machine! In that computer we've got 30,000 state contractors, and we go systematically through them. If they want to do business with the state, they've gotta come through me.' And that's when everybody in the room sort of looked around and went: 'This is not going to end well.'"

He was flying high and Vegas became his favorite landing pad. It turns out Kelly had a big time gambling problem, one he funded through his shady business practices.

According to the second federal indictment against him (to which he also pled guilty), he had rigged the bidding system for the O'Hare contracts, just as rival contractor O'Brien suggested.

Here's the breakdown from a 28-page agreement. Kelly admitted that between 1998 and 2006, he had worked with an insider to steer $8.5 million in O'Hare contracts to his company BCI. He used the proceeds for a variety of personal purposes, which included more than $370,000 in gambling debts and repayment of a $700,000 loan to buy the Blue Ridge mansion he called home. About $450,000 went to pay off the person – not named in the affidavit – who'd helped him rig the bids.

My husband knew this guy was up to no good way back in college.

Blago's father-in-law didn't like him any better. When he finally got the chance, as rumors spread about Kelly's strong-arm fundraising tactics, Dick Mell dropped the bombshell. As he'd already had a falling out with his son-in-law, in the midst of a tirade denouncing him to the press, Mell accused Kelly of outright corruption.

The first indictment was a 12-count set of tax fraud charges. At first, Blago backed his old pal, but that soon changed. The feds were closing in. In January 2009, he pled guilty to the tax charges, and barely a month later he was indicted a 2nd time, in connection with the O'Hare bidding scheme.

His last words at the hospital as they strapped him down for an ambulance transfer were: "It's my life. Tell them they won. Tell them they won." On September 12th it was announced that Kelly was dead.

There is no tragedy in what happened to Kelly or his crony Blago.

Blago, true to his own set of upside down ethics, claimed that the feds drove him to it. As this shameless, self-promoting cheat was plugging his new book, he stated about Kelly: "He refused to lie about someone and not stand up for the truth."

I'd like to make two things clear as prosecutors pointed out:

1) They were not asking Kelly to lie, as Blagojevich suggested, but simply to tell the truth.

2) "The limit is really very ethically simple," said Erickson, retired Cook County circuit and Illinois appellate court judge, "You can bring whatever pressure" as long as you're seeking the truth.

The only disappointment or shame in this story is that the rat got off too easy. He did not go to prison. He did not pay his debt to society.

Instead, he died a fitting death like the rat that he always was, by eating rat poison.

The only regret I have in writing this is that it is perhaps unfair to rats.

The question to ask is why some people believe it would in a way absolve him if he'd done it in order not to rat out a friend. In other words, since when is it honorable for one crook to bail out another crook?

Narcissists have a twisted sense of fairness.

What's OK and What's Not OK...

It's not simply a curiosity to me that people so often make excuses for narcissists. It's an affront.

For example, the extent to which an individual like Chris Kelly went to secure his stronghold goes well beyond one former senior aide's description.

He simply stated that Kelly was passionate and had a genuine, however misguided, desire to do the right thing.

Come on now, who's kidding who? He had a desire to do the right thing? He knew what he was doing. He just didn't care that what he was doing was wrong.

The underlying reason why he didn't care is because he was a narcissist. What is good for the narcissist is good for all.

The direct quote is: "He was a guy who wore his heart on his sleeve and wanted to win and was doing everything he could for the cause," he says. Allow me to tweak this ever so slightly. The only cause Chris Kelly cared about was Chris Kelly.

The quote goes on: "He just lacked political judgment and very clearly lacked an understanding of where the lines were drawn and what's OK and what's not OK."

After reading more quotes from this particular senior aide, I'm beginning to wonder about his sincerity.

One would have to be a genuine idiot to trust the good intentions of a character like Kelly, let alone Blago. That is unless they were as untrustworthy and narcissistic as those two were, or in Blago's case, still is. Scratch a Russian and find a peasant. Scratch a politician and...what was that line from Forrest Gump. Oh yeah: "His legs are strong...as strong as I've ever seen. But his back is as crooked as a politician."

Money is all that ever mattered to the likes of Kelly and Blago and that probably goes for anyone who thinks they were innocent by-standers. I wouldn't trust these people any farther than I could throw them.

"And that's all I have to say about that."

Apart from the Forrest Gump quotes, and personal anecdotes, all previous quotes were taken from: "The Life and Death of Blago Aide Christopher Kelly" by Bryan Smith. It was enlightening.

Loopholes are a narcissist's best friend.

Le Gavage: From Farms to Factories

If the previous story wasn't enough to make you gag, surely this one will.

Shades of narcissism can be found in the way a society treats its animals. The United States is not the only culprit of what many would call animal cruelty. One way to deal with inhumane practices is to ban the sale of food items obtained in ways that are unappetizing.

For example, California has banned the sale of foie gras because of the way it is obtained, through a practice known as "le gavage." However, some chefs there have found a way around the ban. One in particular, who just happens to be French, offers foie gras for free with the price of drinks, charging more for the drinks to make up the difference. She made the argument that other animals are mistreated in the U.S., so why not?

Here's my question: Since when do two wrongs make a right?

I've also heard the excuse that a duck does not have the same gag reflex as a human. Again, I just can't help but smell the narcissism.

For anyone unfamiliar with the practice known as "le gavage," it is the force feeding of ducks so that their livers become enlarged. Even a hamburger joint in California has tried to find a way around the ban on the production and sale of foie gras. They, too, offer their own version of a "complimentary side" of foie gras with one of their specialty burgers. PETA got involved when they realized the side was served on top of the burger just as it had been in pre-ban days. The burger with the "free" foie gras is more expensive than the other burgers on the menu.

I recently watched a program on TV5 Monde called: "Le Village Préféré des Français" and out of 22 villages the one chosen as the favorite village of the French in 2012 was Saint-Cirq-Lapopie in the Region Midi-Pyrénées in Quercy, known for its foie gras and all things duck.

Of course, it's not just the treatment of ducks and chickens that has animal rights activists up in arms. It has long been a problem how veal is obtained and how cattle overall are treated around the world.

Update: At the time of publishing, the California ban on foie gras was lifted...and the story continues.

Narcissism is lack of empathy on steroids.

Temple Grandin

As a spokesperson for all things humane, Temple Grandin stands her ground. She is not only a prominent proponent of animal and human rights but also for autistic person's rights, as she herself is autistic. Many will remember her from the HBO film starring Clare Danes called simply: Temple Grandin.

What stands out in the film of her life, from early development all the way through to her work with cattle and beyond, is her creativity and her uncanny ability for problem solving.

She created designs for curved corrals in order to reduce stress in animals, most notably cattle, on their way to slaughter.

The idea of unnecessary cruelty, although I'm not sure when cruelty is ever necessary, is a favorite topic of hers. Her quest is to promote better treatment of animals even though we use animals for food. She is not a vegetarian and does not advocate that lifestyle choice. Nonetheless, PETA has seen fit to present her with an award for her efforts toward better treatment of animals.

Unnecessary cruelty amounts to nothing less than torture. By finding ways to prevent torture, we show respect. Her methods reflect the respect animals deserve, as she creates ways to limit stress if not outright abuse of animals along the way.

I would call her actions highly empathic. She is not a highly relationship oriented individual due to her autism. She claims it's just not part of her. But what she lacks in that respect, she more than makes up for in her compassion for other living creatures.

She is not married and has no children. (Of course, there are plenty of people who live a more or less celibate life and who do not have autism.) Her case is different, as she displays an extreme ability for compassion combined with ability to affect change for the better.

Most would agree that true altruism does not exist, as there is always something we get out of what we do for others. Her case is no different, as she does speak on the topic of autism and how to handle children with autism. However, she seems to stand out as an example of someone with very little narcissism.

Narcissists do exist. They very often have partners and use those in their closest personal circles to get their way. Their way typically involves only what is good for them and has nothing to do with altruistic pursuits. They keep only those closest to them who serve their needs, fully believing that their needs are the best and most important needs of all.

What's good for the narcissist is good for all. Sacrifices made by others are not important. Suffering endured by other living creatures does not matter. As long as their needs are met and they get their way, it's all good.

I would not expect to find narcissists among animal rights activists. A narcissist is the type that likes to give double standard responses to questions involving le gavage. They will find ways around a ban against animal cruelty rather than find ways to improve treatment of animals to minimize suffering and to treat them with the respect they deserve.

It is my educated guess that they would not find it stressful for cattle to be mistreated at any stage of the process. As for the Milgram Experiment, they would not find it as stressful, if stressful at all, as some did in performing their role as teacher. If anything, they might act like they are affected, if only in order to get something out of it.

Shine a light, different from the one the narcissist is hogging, and you'll uncover the world's ills, if not ill-gotten gains.

Factory Farming: A Pig's Tale

Anyone who practices factory or industrial farming is truly a pig (used only as a figure of speech).

Cruelty, food-borne disease and negative impacts on the environment are perhaps the top three reasons to stop factory farming in favor of other options.

The claim that animals in factory farms are treated no worse than most house pets is simply wrong. Caged and crated, pigs, chickens and veal calves are crammed into spaces barely larger than their own bodies. In order to fit pigs into ever smaller spaces, they actually amputate their tails without the use of anesthesia. If a private citizen confined a dog or cat in such a way and performed surgical procedures without anesthesia, that person would be charged with animal cruelty. And pigs are highly intelligent.

Chickens are kept in such tight spaces that they end up falling into a behavior known as stress-induced cannibalism. Rather than treat them with respect, they are debeaked to prevent them from this practice. I've even seen chickens tethered to stakes in the north Georgia mountains. It sickens me to see the way that chicken farmers treat them. The laws allow for loopholes like an open door (on large covered, overcrowded chicken coops) which lets in just a small amount of sunlight and only for a few minutes at a time. Somehow that is supposed to translate into free range. It pays to know the source. Some suggest certified humane as the appropriate wording for those raised in open air environments.

Veal calves have long been a focus of animal rights activists, as they are prevented from moving around freely, tethered to one spot to prevent normal muscle formation and then cut short on normal life span.

Of course, I could go on for pages describing war-camp-like conditions as inhumane for animals as they once were for humans.

The result of these factory farm conditions---done in the name of increasing profits---is not only a concern for animal welfare. Humans are falling ill, too, as we consume the large quantities of antibiotics, hormones and highly concentrated feed used to sustain these animals.

Thus, formerly lifesaving drugs are becoming useless in combating human disease.

Animal fecal matter contaminates our food, milk and water. This is due to animals in factory farms being infected with pathogens that are transmitted to humans either in the flesh or through carcass contamination at the slaughterhouse.

Animal waste pollutes the land, air and water. Some manure is used to fertilize crops, but most is stored in pits or lagoons and thus becomes a threat to land, air and especially water.

Although measures have been taken and laws passed to curb such unhealthy practices, the CAFO rules (rules governing concentrated animal feeding operations) do not apply to the majority of poultry farms and, unfortunately, do not extend to big processing companies and do not allow for public review of waste management plans for individual farms.

Narcissists thrive on loopholes like these. Laws and bans on animal cruelty mean nothing to them. As long as short term profits continue, they do not focus on changing their methods unless forced to do so. They do not look ahead but rather put profit first---before all else---with little regard for health concerns whether it is for animals, humans or the environment.

Human rights and animal rights are closely tied.
Narcissists do not respect either one.

Monkey Business Right in Your Own Backyard

South Carolina's Farm Animal and Research Protection Act

What exactly does this act protect? Well, it sounds like a legal way around the protection of innocent animals. In other words, it helps local governments to get around animal cruelty bans.

Who's at the "heart" of this act and additional acts that disregard animal rights in the name of big business? According to what I've read, it is Senator Verdin, Chairman of the Agriculture and Natural Resources Committee.

Who is Senator Verdin? He is the son of a veterinarian and the owner of Verdin's Farm and Garden Center. Both the SC Veterinarian Association and the SC Farm Bureau named him Legislator of the Year in 2006 and 2007, respectively. He was given the highest award from Future Farmers of America – "The Honorary American FFA Degree."

What makes him deserving of such honors? He has sponsored laws and amendments to make

71

sure the South Carolina SPCA (and other such organizations) has no arrest powers under the state's Animal Cruelty Act. For example, it allows for the Livestock and Poultry Regulations to prohibit local governments from passing laws to protect poultry.

Such laws do not protect animals. Instead, the lack of transparency furthers potential for animal abuse. For example, there is no way to discover what is happening to monkeys coming into South Carolina. Are they destined for zoos or for research labs?

What do research labs do with monkeys in South Carolina? At one facility, AGI (Alpha Genesis Inc.) located in Yemassee and Hampton, they are tortured, some with probes in their brains. With half of their skull cut away in order to insert the probes, their brain waves can be monitored while they perform tasks, such as puzzles, to get food. I have a better idea. Let's probe the politician(s) instead.

A narcissist's sentiments are only skin deep.

Cruelty in the Cosmetics Industry: Some Bunny Always Pays

Over 80% of the world still allows cruel and unnecessary testing on animals such as rabbits, rats, mice and guinea pigs to take place for the sake of cosmetics. This includes the USA and Asia.

China actually requires that cosmetics be tested on animals.

Whether it is true or not, the most often cited reason for not using alternative methods to test for safety is that they do not always work for more innovative products. Nonetheless, the EU has recently tightened controls to prohibit the sale of cosmetics originating in places that do not follow humane guidelines, i.e. a ban on newly animal-tested cosmetics.

Human safety is not the only issue. Humane testing is equally important to many who believe how a product is produced also matters.

The issue of implementation is still a concern. Because loopholes exist, and because some are willing to forego humane treatment for profits, labels for cruelty free cosmetics are about as clear as free range chicken and cage free eggs. Just as "certified humane" seems to be the clearest in the food industry, so the leaping bunny symbol seems to represent that "no animal was used in the testing of this product."

The use of rabbits to test eye make-up is the most ubiquitous example found in cruelty free cosmetics campaigns. I taught issues related to the use of animals, particularly bunnies, in writing classes as long ago as the 1980s. I repeated the same examples as ethical issues in the marketing classes I taught beyond the year 2000. That's far too long for scientists not to have come up with better solutions. And that's just my personal experience and awareness. Now, at least, it seems some progress has been made.

The recently tightened ban in the EU is the result of a law passed twenty years ago.

For anyone who is unaware of the type of testing used on animals like rabbits, the following description should prove enlightening, if not sickening. It is called the Draize test after FDA toxicologist John Draize. Commonly an albino rabbit is used, but other animals are also used, including dogs.

From the PETA Factsheet: The Draize eye- and skin-irritation/corrosion test dates back to the 1940s.(3) During this test, rabbits are often immobilized in full-body restraints while a substance is dripped or smeared into their eyes or onto their shaved skin. Laboratory technicians then record the damage at specific intervals for hours or days. Rabbits may suffer swollen eyelids, irritated and cloudy eyes, and inflamed skin, and in the case of irreversible corrosive damage, they may endure ulcers, bleeding, bloody scabs, or blindness.

The scoring of eye and skin damage in the Draize test is highly subjective, and therefore, different laboratories—and even different tests within the same laboratory—often yield different results. In addition, rabbits' eyes are anatomically and physiologically different from and tend to have stronger reactions to chemicals than humans' eyes. One

study found that the Draize test "grossly overpre-
dicted the effects that could be seen in the human
eye," and another concluded that the test "does
not reflect the eye irritation hazard for man."(4) In
contrast, a clinical skin patch test conducted on
human volunteers has been shown to produce
skin-irritation data that are "inherently superior
to that given by a surrogate model, such as the
rabbit."(5)

No bunny deserves that.

For a narcissist, conflict is easily resolved. Out of sight, out of mind.

Blood Diamonds Revisited

Then again, why should animal abuse in China surprise us, when child abuse is still so prevalent there and around the developing world? Children's rights have a long way to go as do workers' rights both within China's borders and without. When they do business with Africa in places like Congo, they are not alone in taking advantage of some of the poorest people in the world. Nonetheless, they are still guilty of exploiting them.

Reminiscent of the small scale diamond mines in Sierra Leone, child labor exists in copper and cobalt mines that supply Chinese companies in Congo. The children who work there are known as "creuseurs" or diggers; that is, they dig the ore by hand and carry sacks of ore on their backs for sale to Chinese companies.

The percentages are high. It is estimated that over 60% of Katanga's processing plants are owned by Chinese companies and 90% of the region's minerals go to China. So, when asked the question why single out China as the poster child for propaganda against child labor, just look at the numbers. No matter which other countries are also involved in abuses, two or more wrongs don't make a right.

According to one report, approximately 80,000 child laborers under the age of 15, that is about 40% of all miners, were supplying ore to Chinese companies in this African region.

All that glitters is not gold, at least not for families engaged in the extraction of the mineral in West Africa. In countries such as Mali, third largest exporter of gold in Africa, somewhere between 20,000 and 40,000 children work in what is known as artisanal mining. What a pretty word to describe backbreaking toil. 'Artisanal' is usually reserved for some kind of jewelry or bread making on a small scale, complete with the marketing images of sparklingly upscale displays of the artists' wares.

Instead, artisanal mining (locally known as "orpaillage") involves children as young as 6 who work with their families. These children along with their families suffer chronic exposure to toxic chemicals, including mercury. The poor work practices have long term health consequences for the children, as well as environmental consequences, as tons of mercury are released every year into local rivers, groundwater and lakes.

Gold is an important export for both Mali and Ghana. For Mali, it is the 2nd largest earner of export revenue. For many poor families with children it is the primary, if not only, source of income.

Conflict diamonds might no longer be used to supply arms for revolution in war torn Africa, but they are still a source of worker exploitation and child abuse. Approximately one million diamond diggers in Africa (Sierra Leone in particular) earn less than a dollar a day. Unsafe conditions and practices often result in injury and even death among a work force that includes children.

Even if laws do exist, they are rarely enforced, making small scale diggers (who are unlicensed and lack access to global markets) subject to middle men, who buy up the diamonds at below market prices.

The Butterfly Effect

Whether it is the exploitation of mine workers or farmers around the world, we've all heard stories of enforcing laws that punish those who would act in environmentally concerned and responsible ways. A very recent news story out of France featured one organic winegrower who outright refused to spray for a certain bacterial disease of the vine called la flavescence dorée. The winegrower's argument is that the treatment does not fit the disease any more than it seems the punishment would fit the "crime" of organic means over poisons. The insecticide solution just doesn't work.

The fact of the matter is that GMOs, or pesticides GMO crops are bred to resist, take a toll on nature. Human beings are not separate from nature. We are a part of nature. The way we treat the land and people who work the land reveals a lot about human nature when it comes to profit over purpose. Unfortunately, the overriding purpose has been for quantity over quality rather than the other way around.

The result of many of these misguided deeds is a spiraling out of control healthcare system. People are encouraged to consume what is not good for them by a system that has made them slaves to healthcare largely through insurance company driven scare tactics. It's this buy now, pay later attitude that is spreading around the world. Less physical activity, mixed with low caliber fast food and a sedentary lifestyle - tied to computer activities rather than outdoor sports, is a growing trend. Due to such changes in culture, places like France are starting to look a lot more like places in the U.S. in terms of the younger generations. Modification of diet is not the only concern. It is not only our behavior that needs to be modified but the behavior of the monster that feeds on us.

Unless something happens to change the trend, or we intend to supply our own homegrown versions of just about everything found in our supermarkets, we are at the mercy of corporate giants like Monsanto. Although I applaud justice against the pesticide giant...I refer to the case of the Frenchman who won the lawsuit after being poisoned by exposure to Monsanto's Lasso...I'd rather be healthy.

A narcissist is a dangerous master of disguise.
The disguise changes all the time.

Jacques et le haricot magique (or Jack and the Beanstalk)

In 1807, Benjamin Tabart wrote the moralistic version of "Jack and the Beanstalk" that we have all come to know and love. Other variants of the tale exist.

Just as with real-life situations, there are two sides to every story. In the case of Jack, a closer version of the original story was made popular in 1890 by Joseph Jacobs. It is as close to the narrative as we can hope to get, for the lack of moralizing.

Jack, it seems, was originally a trickster and appeared in other so-called "Jack tales." But in Tabart's version, Jack is an innocent young lad, who lives alone with his mother. They are poor and need to sell their cow (who stopped giving milk) in order to survive. At the market, Jack runs into an old man, who talks him into a trade: the cow in exchange for magic beans. Distraught by his foolish act, Jack's mom throws the beans out the window. By morning, there is a giant beanstalk – which Jack decides to climb. When he reaches the top, he encounters a giant who wants to eat him and the giant's wife who conspires with him to outsmart her husband by helping Jack - not only to rob the giant of his golden coins but also of his golden harp and goose who lays the golden eggs.

All of this is okay because the giant is, after all, a villain. It's the Robin Hood effect that Tabart's version presents to his readers. And that makes it okay to rob and even kill the giant, especially since the backstory is that the giant had robbed and killed Jack's father.

Not so in Jacob's version. He gives no justification, as there was none given in the version he heard (told to him as a child). It fact, his version vilifies Jack.

Countless versions have followed. Some go back to earlier times. Perhaps most interesting is the tale, reputedly of Persian origin, called: "The

Gourd and the Palm-tree." Reminiscent of an ancient Northern European belief in a "world tree connecting Earth to Heaven," that one speaks to all things in moderation. It tells of the dangers of a fast growing gourd vine. Although it sprouts seeds and outgrows a mature palm, it ultimately dies in the frost.

Everyone likes the stories from their childhood best. And, at the risk of moralizing, the version I like best is the one where good triumphs over evil. Sometimes the giant pretends to be something else, something worthy of our sympathy and support. That goes back to the saying that the greatest trick the devil ever pulled was in getting people to believe he didn't exist.

The truth lies between good and evil, somewhere between Jack being a hero and Jack being a villain, and other Jack tales like: Jack be nimble...Jack be quick...Jack jumped over the candlestick.

Even if somewhere along the way, such variants as Jack being the hero lost their luster, lost their mass appeal, or lost their popularity, in the end it is always Jack who slays the giant and lives happily ever after.

How's that for a bottom line - Monsanto - fee fi fo fum.

ABOUT THE AUTHOR

Kim Taylor is a former professor of languages and marketing. With an educational background that includes three post graduate degrees (MA in French Literature, MA in Linguistics and MBA) she has taught at major universities in the US and abroad.

As a Fulbright Award recipient to the College of Music and Dramatic Arts, she was involved in providing translations for various performances while living in Bratislava, Slovakia. Her interest in business practices sparked during a concurrent assignment to a college of economics. As a matter of course, she used Russian and German in every-day life overseas. Her linguistic skills allowed her to adapt readily to diverse Slavic languages of the region.

Her background in French began even earlier and her travels to the French speaking world are numerous. She has lived and worked in France as an English language consultant at a prestigious international school outside of Paris.

She currently resides in Savannah, GA with her husband, a well-known landscape architect, where she is focused on her writing, consulting and import fragrance business.